PRESENTED TO:

_____

BY:

_____

DATE:

_____

My Heart Speaks Through My Pen

*An exposure of the heart through story and poetry
......for reason to encourage.*

KAREN D. TRUETT

WESTBOW
PRESS®
A DIVISION OF THOMAS NELSON
& ZONDERVAN

WestBow Press books may be ordered through booksellers or by contacting:

WestBow Press
A Division of Thomas Nelson & Zondervan
1663 Liberty Drive
Bloomington, IN 47403
www.westbowpress.com
1 (866) 928-1240

ISBN: 978-1-4908-7710-5 (sc)
ISBN: 978-1-4908-7711-2 (e)

Library of Congress Control Number: 2015906210

Print information available on the last page.

WestBow Press rev. date: 08/17/2015

My Heart Speaks Through My Pen

KAREN D. TRUETT

Table of Contents

To my dear family and friends, I love you and I'm so grateful for you. Each of you makes my life a little sweeter.

Introduction

The first poem that I wrote was in my mini-van on the way home from Dallas to Sherman in 1995. I prayed and asked God to give me an idea for a "welcome home" gift for my brother. I wanted it to be a gift that wouldn't get shoved to the back of the shelf or drawer. I wanted it to be special. Then, all of a sudden, words just started coming to my mind. I started grabbing napkins, scraps of paper, whatever I could find to write on. The first poem "New Beginnings" was finished by the time I got home.

★★★★★★★★★★★

Most poems in this book were written for someone specifically as I thought or prayed for them.

Some….are an expression from my heart that I thought would stay in my notebook, never being read by anyone but me.

Some…are a sort of gentle correction - somehow to get me back on track.

As I gathered the scraps of paper I have written on throughout the years and typed them out, trying to organize them, my hope is that if anyone ever reads them, they would be comforted or encouraged somehow.

Fresh New Beginnings

Fresh new beginnings are a good place to start
As long as you keep God in your heart.
Things can be good – yes they can!
If we follow God's leading and take God's hand.

We can try on our own, but it will never work
Our own way brings disappointment, sometimes sorrow and hurt.
And if life sometimes gets too hard to bear.
Remember, God loves you and said he'd be there.

So bow down before Him and worship His name
And your life will never be the same.
Spend time before Him each day and each night
And he will fill you with His power, His love and His might.

Change can be good if we start out the right way
Be strong in the Lord and stand firm in the faith.
So when you can't see God's detailed plan through
Be led by His Spirit and just keep pressing through.

If things get rough, and sometimes they do
Keep reading the Word and stay fresh and anew.
And don't run away if things do get hard
Draw strength from the Lord and you will go far.

Don't wither away as some people do
Stay fresh and alive!
So God can use you!

After saying harsh words to my husband, I stood at the kitchen cabinet as he walked out the back door......

The thought came to me, "What if those were the last words he ever heard me say?"

My heart was broken. I got down on my knees in the kitchen and asked God to forgive me. That's when the words of the poem "No Regrets" came to me. I stood at the cabinet and finished the poem as the words flowed from my heart to the paper.

I think this was one of those "gentle correction" poems for me to get me back on track.

(No Regrets – Page 14)

No Regrets

Oh, how wonderful life is when you have no regrets!

As I read God's word daily and sought after His face,
I was filled with His joy and His love, given His grace.
I could love others the way He wanted me to
But it was because of His love that I was able to.

I spent time with God daily, and that's how it should be
If we are to live life victoriously.

I saw life with such beauty and happiness then
But it was because of the time I was spending with Him.
You see, the love of God makes all things look bright,
And without this love, nothing seems right.

Then one day death came unexpectedly
Though ready or not, it had to be.
But even through sadness there was a happiness I had
That I didn't have to be sorry for something I'd said.

But as the years went by, a busyness crept in
One that was stealing my time with Him.
Then I was reminded one day as I spoke with harsh words
If today was their last, I have filled them with hurt.

I spoke not in love, because my well had run dry.
It has to be filled with His love, not mine.
Our love is not good enough and this now I know
It's from the well of Living Water that this love must flow.

God says, death and life are in the power of the tongue
Be careful what you say, what you say will be done.

So not wanting to continue to go on this way,
I got down on my knees and began to pray.
"God, please forgive me. I don't want to say,
Anything to hurt anyone – like I did today."

God said His mercy is new every morning.
And because of His forgiveness, we can keep going.
So which words will you choose, which path will you take?
"I love you, honey," or "not now, go away!"

Every day will come and we'll have to choose
If you walk in love, it's up to you.
Choose this day which path you will take
I want to choose life and ask God for His grace.

Today, remember what's important, and don't get upset
So tomorrow can come and you'll have no regrets.

So take time to do or take time to say
Whatever it takes to love God's way.
So when this time is gone you can look back and say,
I have "No Regrets," I am happy today.

Oh, how wonderful life is when you have no regrets!

So Much More Than That

The Lord did bless me with someone
That I did call my dad
But he lost his life to a heart attack
And I was very sad.

Anytime a life is lost
Too early in the game
You can know that one thing is for sure
The devil is to blame.

The day did come that I did marry
And Truett became my name
But little did I know what all was in store
There was so much that I would gain.

Although there are many in this family
That mean so much to me
I'll speak only of one man
That I met in this family.

I met a man who cared for me
Just like I was his own
And through the years I grew to love him
More than he'll ever know.

There was a time, however
When I drank out of his coke
I didn't know until years later
But it became a family joke.

There are so many things that I admire
About this wonderful man
He's honest, faithful, noble, and strong
He knows just when to stand.

He's one I'd call immoveable
He's proved this many times
But most of all he's a God-fearing man
And I know he's changed many lives.

Sometimes it's hard for me to say
Exactly how I feel
But through this poem I hope I'll show
My love for him is real.

This man is my father-in-law
But he's SO MUCH MORE THAN THAT
He is someone special
Someone I'd be proud – to call my very own dad!

THE BEAUTY OF THE ROSE

My dear mother, you're like the rose, so beautiful to me.
So great the beauty of that rose the thorns I do not see.
Though some may look at a rose, and see just thorns are there.
Others look and only see the beauty God put there.

See God is working in us all
To trim away our thorns.
It's only if we let Him though
That we will not get torn.

Torn up by life's problems
That we try to solve ourselves.
That God can handle, If we let Him
Just fine by Himself.

The rose is our example
To see God's in control.
He can take the thorns of life
And make things beautiful like the rose.

Mom, You're like the rose, so beautiful to me.

Love,
Karen

OUR MEMA

Our mema is so special
We love her very much.
Our time with her special
So gentle is her touch.

To be with her is unlike being
With anybody else.
We have lots and lots of fun with her
And enjoy the stories she tells.

Mom likes the talks!
Em' likes the games!
Jake likes the hikes!
Dad likes the biscuits she makes!

Mema, we thank you for the love
That you have for our Lord.
We've learned a lot by watching you
Obey His Holy Word.

The life you live
Will always give
Such happiness to us.

From "mother-may-I"
To "mema's milk"!
WE LOVE YOU VERY MUCH!

While driving home after running errands, the thought came to sit and write a note to a loved one when I got home. I didn't know what to say, so I put it off a few days, but the thought would not leave me.

Finally, I just got a pen and a piece of paper and went to sit on my front porch.

When I sat there ready, with pen and paper....these words came.

(A fan for Jesus – Page 22)

A fan for Jesus? or A fool for the devil?

I'd rather be a fan for Jesus
I'd rather be peculiar for the Lord
Than the "dummy of the day"
A fool for the devil
Trouble's all the devil has in store.

To really walk with the Lord
To be His true disciple
Means we have to take a stand
And be different from other people.

It's those that stood out
And chose to be different
All this in the Bible we read.

It was people like Daniel
And the three Hebrew men
These kind always receive.

What kind of person is this you say
That would receive from God
In this special way.

It's the person who "dares to be different"
And doesn't care what others may say.

I think of the man named Bartimaeus
Who yelled so loud for the Master
Must have seemed strange to so many
But he could see from that moment after.

What about Peter when he walked on the water
What are his friends going to think?
He was walking just fine – til he took his eyes off Jesus
That's when he started to sink!

There's a lesson to be learned
In this word from the Lord.
And this decision – only you can make.

To be used by God
And to see special miracles
It's a choice YOU have to make!

Now the devil will tell us
We don't have to be different
Just serve God any ole' way.
The devil – He is a liar!
YOU must choose whom you'll serve this day!

I'll tell you right now, that there won't be many
Who will choose this narrow road.
I once heard a saying, "birds fly in flocks,
But Eagles fly alone."

There may be times when it seems
That you are walking alone.
But He gave us His Word
He'd never forsake us
Nor ever leave us alone.

We all have the same choice
All on the same level
    To be a fan for Jesus...
            or a fool for the devil.

Seasons

A season is a time in life
A time that's sure to change.
But the special people that cross our paths
Their memories always remain.

The season in my life
That I needed a special friend to fill.
Was you — Sonya
I won't forget — I never will.

The times you listened
I could always tell,
What I was feeling
You also felt.

On this journey on the earth
There are jobs He'll have us do.
I believe the job to help me through
That job was assigned to you.

As sure as the season we're in
Is about to change.
I know there is a certain thing
That will always stay the same.

And that's the memory of a friend
Who I've had lots of fun with.
Whether it was walking at the mall
Or eating El Chico chips!

During this season
We all know
We celebrate our Lord.
But I always look forward to the next
To see what he has in store.

I thank the Lord for a beautiful life
And for all it's changing seasons.
I thank the Lord a lot for you
I have so many reasons.

MY MOUTH WAS MADE FOR PRAISE

You made my mouth to praise You
But I often use it in different ways.
Sometimes for gossip,
Sometimes for criticism
A lot of the time just to complain.

I don't take the time to thank You
Or praise You like I should.
Or take the time to lift people up
Or use my mouth the way I should.

One minute I use my mouth for blessing
The next from my mouth a cursing will flee.
And in the Bible, James 3 verse 10
He said, "brethren this ought not to be."

The right things have to be in the heart
Before the right things can come out of the mouth.
But time has to be spent in the Word - with the Father
Or nothing but idle words will come out.

God says we will have to give an account
For every idle word we say.
Lord help my words be pleasing to You
Set a watch before my mouth today.

Lord, I ask for Your forgiveness
For using this instrument, my mouth, in any wrong way.
Father help me fill my heart with Your words
So I can speak the truth boldly each day.

Lord, I want You to use my mouth
For whatever purpose You choose.
I'll do my best to use this instrument
To only bring glory to You.

      ......because

            .....my mouth was made for praise.

A True Giver and His Great Reward

A true Giver is someone who gives
Wanting nothing in return.
No pats, no plaques, no "adda-boys"
No recognition wants to be heard.

For if you seek such recognition
As found here on the earth.
There will be no reward in Heaven waiting
For you have received it all on earth.

The Lord said be careful when you give
Don't announce it unto men.
For if you truly give unto Him
Only He should know it then.

So let's remember as we give
Let's give as unto the Lord.
For waiting here and in Heaven
Will be our Great Reward!

TAKING THE TIME

Time is a gift given from God
To us to give to others!
****

Will we spend it only on ourselves
Or find the time to share?
For those who are really looking
The opportunity is always there.

Jesus took time for the blind man
When others told him to be quiet.
Jesus took time for the children
And told the disciples not to deny them.

Jesus always took the time
To do what others wouldn't.
He spent time with all kinds of people
Even when they thought He shouldn't.

He said My ways are not your ways
And your thoughts are not like Mine.
I love those who you would not
And yes – with them – I will spend time.

If you give a cup of cold water
You will be rewarded.
Give and it shall be given to you
Pressed down and running over.

You see when you give something to another
You're not only giving to them.
God said when you do it for the least of these
You're really doing it for Him.

FORGIVE ME

Please forgive me for all the times
I've hurt you with my words.
I just want to share the things that frustrate me
But I never mean to hurt.

There are plenty of things that I
Have left – many times – undone.
But never once have you mentioned them
Or complained – no not one.

Thanks for being understanding
The way I want to be.
I want us to respect each other
I'll pray for you – you pray for me.

I know you work very hard
And you're very good to me.
I'm very grateful that your mine
I know we're meant to be.

I don't usually watch Oprah, but one night I was flipping channels and came across Oprah interviewing a woman that had lost her son to a motorcycle crash. My heart ached for this lady. I prayed for her as I sat on the couch. Four words that she said just kept going over and over in my head. . . . "Just five more minutes."

This is my least favorite poem, but the words came for a reason. Maybe to remind us to pray for our loved ones or for the ones that have lost theirs.

(Just Five More Minutes – Page 34)

Just Five More Minutes

I heard a story about
A woman who lost her son
It was in a motorcycle wreck
He was eighteen, very young.

She talked about the night he died
And the decision she had to make
Should she keep things as they are
Or through her son, give life and donate.

* * * * * * * *

She chose that night to share her son
To give others more time with their loved ones.

* * * * * * * * *

Even though she was very sad
You could tell she was very strong.
I know she must have been a Christian
Only that kind of strength comes from God.

But there was one thing that she said
That made me stop and think
She said "If I had just five more minutes with him."
You could tell her heart began to sink.

I thought to myself — "Why did she want just five?"
Was it to apologize, or to tell him something?
Or just to be with him one last time.

Lord, give this mother strength and comfort
That only You can give
Help her have a happy life
Until they meet again.

Lord, protect my children, family and friends
From the weapons formed against us
But also let us live our lives
As if we had "Just Five More Minutes"

No weapons formed against us will prosper. (Isa 54:17)

WHISPERS FROM HEAVEN

Whispers from Heaven can change your life
It takes but one word to shed the light.
.........The light on a problem
         Or an unsure path
         The answer to all
         Is within our grasp
The Lord says listen, and I will speak
Whether on a plane or a mountain peak.
         God can speak like thunder
         Or whisper in a breeze
         What He has to say
         Is all we'll ever need

         The whisper is God's voice
         You can't afford not to hear
         Be still and just listen
         He who has ears let him hear
He'll whisper while you're reading the Word
Even during the night His voice can be heard.
         Whatever the need
         He has the answer
         But we must be still
         And get into His presence

Lord, anoint our ears to hear what the Spirit of the Lord is saying
to us. Amen

YES, I AM REAL

I am real
I know just who you are
I know what you're doing right now
I'm never, ever far.

I've been there in your past
I know what you've been through
I know where you will go from here
But the choice is up to you.

There is a road to Heaven
There is a road to Hell
But only one road can be chosen
And both places are very real.

I have a plan for you.
I really need your help
Please choose the road that leads to me
So others won't burn in Hell.

I had to go through things that hurt
Just like you have on this earth
And when things don't go good
Don't do what you want – Do what you should.

This is the way you follow me
By forgiving others – it will set you free
I want you to know I love you, and I always will
I am God – And, yes, I AM REAL.

Anyone who knows me knows that being in front of people is not my favorite thing to do.

My Sunday school teacher was going to be out of town and asked if I would be willing to fill in that week, I said I would. I needed help!

As I was studying what I was going to share that week, I prayed and asked God for help. The words of this poem came. It was added to the lesson. I didn't realize that the Word of God was so many things.

. . . . .It's everything.

(The Word – Page 40)

THE WORD

The Word is God
The Word is alive
The Word is water
The Word is seed.

The Word is precious
The Word is pure
The Word is our hope
It's the only words we should speak.

The Word is a lamp
The Word is a light
The Word is health
The Word is life.

The Word is truth
The Word is faithful
The Word is near
The Word is joy.

The Word is quick
The Word is sharp
The Word is powerful
It can also destroy!

The Word is God's will, it is settled in Heaven
The Word we must use it, it is our weapon!

In the beginning was the Word......

John 1:1

IT WON'T BE LONG

It won't be long
Until I come
Back to the earth
To take you home.

So be watching!
Stay awake!
For when I come
It will be too late.

Too late to repent, too late to change
For those who aren't ready, they'll have to remain.

Too late to pray for those who were lost
For those I died for on the cross.

NOW IS THE TIME
To know my Word
And to share with those who haven't heard.

Pray for those whose hearts are hard
Pray that they will see
It is your witness and your prayers
That will lead them all to Me.

I AM COMING
It won't be long.

NO SURPRISE TO ME

Your life may sometimes be full of surprises
You're not sure how things will be,
But I am the God of all creation
Nothing is a surprise to Me.

I know the path that I have planned for you
Way before you were even born.
I've seen the times that you have struggled
When problems have left you worn.

But there is a path that is easy
There is a burden (load) that is light,
There is a place that is peaceful
There is a way that is right.

I have the way that is perfect!
You must find out that way through My Word.
You will learn so many new things
But many things you've already heard.

The key is to do the things that I say
And not be a hearer only.
There are blessings for those who do my will
Right now on earth – not just in Heaven only.

Read My Word and pray everyday
Take your family to church.
You'll know how to live and to love one another
Just by putting Me first.

In this world there will be troubles
But on the cross I conquered each one.
And through the faith that I have given you
You too can overcome.

So don't be afraid of the days ahead
Start every day on your knees.
So that I can teach you the way you should go
I promise I'll never leave.

Through My

. . . . . . I see the good

Kitchen Window

that God has done.

THROUGH MY KITCHEN WINDOW

Through my kitchen window
Are some of the most beautiful things I've seen.
The dew drops on the flowers
The sun rays coming through the trees.

The squirrels that gather, the doves that coo
The beautiful birds that sing.
I see the trees that surround and hover
As the sun glistens on each leaf.

EARLY IN THE MORNING IS MY FAVORITE TIME OF DAY!

It seems that early in the morning
You can hear the sounds so clear.
I'll just sit real still and listen
To see what I can hear.

I hear each bird sing so sweetly
A beautiful different song.
The hummingbird even makes her sound
With her wings buzzing right along.

The squirrels, they make a little barking sound
Who knows what they say.
The rabbits – they're just quite
As they scamper on their way.

The butterflies – they flutter
With color on their wings.
I've even seen baby birds
Trying out their wings.

I've seen so many beautiful things
But this is only one.
The view THROUGH MY KITCHEN WINDOW
I see the good that God has done.

I Prayed for You Today…..

I thank the Lord for who you are
And who you're going to be
The path that He leads us on
Is sometimes hard to see.

Sometimes it's just taking a step
That's all we know to do
Whatever He says – just obey
And He'll provide for you.

His ways are not our ways
He doesn't think the way we do
Kneel, pray and listen
He'll tell you what to do.

God – He is trustworthy
He's there with you right now
He'll lead you where you need to go
Even if you don't know how.

Sometimes things look real bad
Just keep your eyes on Him
Remember Peter – he had a choice
It was either walk or swim!

We also have to choose
What we are going to believe
The millions of voices around us
Speaking doubt, fear and defeat?

Or is it going to be what God says
Is it His Words we'll believe?
He said that he came that we might have life
And life ABUNDANTLY!

We have to be patient, though
As He's working things out for us
Sometimes we don't see Him working
Guess that's why He calls it TRUST.

Just like a movie you've seen before
And you know how it will end
He's delivered many before us
He's the same now as then.

"True Treasures"

True treasures are usually hidden
They must be searched for to find.
One thing that makes them so valuable
Is that they are rare or "one of a kind".

There are the treasures that come from the earth
There are some that come from the sea.
Then there are the treasures that
come straight from Heaven
That were given from God's hands to me.

Among these treasures are many things
That I've come to hold so dear.
I'm thankful for all He has given me
There has been so much down through the years.

These treasures are my children
The "right spouse", a special friend.
Having a family that loves me
This can only be given from Him.

I wouldn't mind having the treasures
That come from the earth or the sea,
But it's my family and friends that surround me
These treasures are worth more to me.

As I feel the love that they've given me
Their sweet faces, of each, I behold.
They're worth more to me and could never be replaced
By the choicest silver or finest gold.

So I'd like to let you know
Just how much you mean to me
You are one of those "true treasures"
That means so much to me.

This poem is written for those special people
in my life. I love you so very much!

QUESTIONS OF THE HEART

Lord, I have so many questions
I don't want to even ask.
For fear I would disrespect You
Or nullify prayers – prayed in the past.

My heart is broken about many things
But I am grateful for many things too.
I want You to be more real to me
Please show me what to do.

When I was seven, I remember
I gave my life to You.
I know I have not lived it perfect
But my desire is to always please You.

I know You really chose me first
That's what it says in Your word.
Your way is the way I wanted to go
It was You I wanted to serve.

There have been times I've tried to encourage
Others when they're down.
I'll try to share with them Your word
It's the only thing that I've believed - could turn it all around.

I wondered – does this all really matter
Or am I giving them false hope.
Unless You're truly real to me
How can I help them know.

But when I look back on my life
At times that weren't so good.
I can't deny that You were there
It was there by me You stood.

I want more than I've ever had before
I don't want You to seem so far away.
Be real to me – Be MY God
Come to me today.

Please answer the Questions of my Heart

Respectfully,

Karen

"A VESSEL OF HONOR"

What is your job
While on the earth?
A doctor, a lawyer
A farmer that tills the dirt?

We are each called to do a job
That He's assigned to us.
But many don't heed to that call
We just don't put Him first.

Each job is important
To make it all just work.
We have to ask which one is ours
There is a reason – we must search.

But as I thought about our Pastor
And what he's assigned to do.
I pictured this beautiful, golden vessel
What he carries inside is truth.

The truth is Jesus the Light of the world
The hope for every generation.
When we come in contact with these vessels
We get a taste of a little bit of Heaven.

These vessels they contain
The presence of Almighty God.
When they're tipped, He pours out
And His love is shed abroad.

His presence may just touch
That one on the street.
Or it may pour out to the nations
Every need He wants to meet.

It has to be an honorable vessel
To carry Him inside.
The contents are very valuable
Where It's holy, He will abide.

Pastor, I know we all are vessels
And should carry His love too.
But this is just what I saw
When we ran into you.

Thank you, Pastor, for answering the call
The job you were assigned to do.
I saw a golden, honorable vessel
That vessel, pastor, was you.

A SOUL THAT'S LOST FOREVER
(a soul separated from God)

A soul that's lost forever
Is a soul that wasn't reached.
Did we just not see them?
Or did we just not teach?

Was it me? Was it you?
That should have reached out to that one.
To rescue them from the devil's clutch
And from eternal damnation.

There are those who choose to turn
And walk away from God.
But there are those who just don't know
Lord, did I do my job?

To teach them there is ONLY ONE WAY
To receive eternal life.
Through confessing and believing
In the Blood of Jesus Christ.

I don't think about how bad it is
For a soul to be lost.
Until you look into the eyes of darkness
Of someone who is lost.

The eyes seem to be
The windows to the soul.
You can see if life is there
Or death – which is as black as coal.

It doesn't seem as real
Until someone you love can't see.
The one that has been leading them
To a place no one wants to be.

It's a place of confusion
A place that seems so deep.
Deep into the darkness
Where the pestilence do creep.

It's a place they'll always hurt
It's a place of no return.
It's a place they'll always thirst
It's a place they'll always burn.

It is hell – and we must rescue them!
From that dreadful, awful place.
We must lead them to Heaven
A place entered, through faith – by grace.

We must help them to that place
Where there is peace and rest.
A place where there is always life
IN GOD'S PRESENCE – is God's best.

There are many souls that are left
We must get to them in time.
To rescue them from eternal death
We must lead them to God's Son.

A soul that is lost forever
Is a soul separated from God.
We must be the one's to close that gap
Or forever they'll be lost.

-    PRAY

Help Me Care Like You Care

Help me care like You care
I don't love them like You do
Teach me, show me, change my heart
So, that I will be able to.

There are so many that suffer
Even those who carry Your name
Lord, help me die, so You can live
Through me to heal their pain.

I've walked with You a long long time
But am I all You want me to be?
If I'm not — I yield to You
Make me everything You want me to be.

I know that time is short
Just show me what to do
Help me see what you see
Lord, help me care like You.

Down by....
The Water's Edge

Down by the water's edge
Is a place of peace and rest
It's a place of restoration
It's a place where you'll be blessed.

It's a place that you can come
Anytime of day
But it's better if you come by first
Before you go your way.

For at this place you'll receive
Strength for every task
It's really easy all you do
Is simply come and ask.

Sometimes we're too busy
We just hurry on our way
We don't think there's time to stop
In our busy day.

Then we find ourselves
Not knowing what to do
If you stop for a while
He'll make it clear to you.

It's the One who leads you by the water
That shows you what to do
It's our Lord and Savior, Jesus Christ
Who will comfort and lead you.

On the way down to the waters
There are pastures, Oh so green
You are lead by someone
Who will give you all you need.

So take some time
To simply pray
This is what He said
Take His hand and He'll lead you...

down by. . . .

the water's edge.

psalm 23

KEEP TRUSTING IN ME

Keep trusting in Me
With all of your heart.
Keep trusting in Me
And don't fall apart.

You ask where I am
It doesn't seem like I'm there.
Don't doubt what I said
I said I'd be there.

Forever and always
Until the end of the Earth.
I'll be beside you
Through the disappointments and hurts.

A season is a space
In the dispensation of time.
This one will soon pass
As the sun's sure to shine.

These times have a reason
They're not clear to you now.
One day you'll look back
And I'll explain to you how.

Experience holds lessons
That no school can teach.
The things that are learned
You can pass on – or keep.

What you pass on will help others
When they're going through.
That season in their life
That's hard for them too.

So keep pressing onward
Hold your head high!
Do all that I've told you
You'll reap in due time.

Things will soon change
Like I've planned them to be.
Don't ever quit
Keep trusting in Me!

WHEN YOUR BACK'S AGAINST THE WALL

When your back's against the wall
And you don't know which way to turn.
Keep on looking upward
If you look down, you'll just see dirt.

For when we look up
It is the Light we see.
It is the light from His sweet face
Looking back at you and me.

There's so much in the Light
That we don't even see.
But the light from His presence
Is everything we need.

It will illuminate our path
When we can't see which way to go.
It will strengthen our inner most being
When we are feeling low.

Even natural sunlight
Promotes good life and health.
How much more our Heavenly Father's light
Will give out when we need help.

We must stay in the rays
Of His Heavenly Light.
It will chase away the darkness
It will make all wrong things right.

So when we feel our back is pressed
So hard against the wall.
He said He'd show us the way out
He said He'd answer when we call.

HOW LONG MUST I WAIT ?

How long must I wait
For what I've believed
To come to pass?

You said when I have
A need for something
All I had to do was ask.

I have asked
And I am waiting
I have waited a long, long time.

Lord, if I'm in error
About anything
Quickly! Put me back in line.

My desire in life
Is to be happy
And see my family happy too.

I have no hope
In anything else
All my hope I've put in You.

Please show me if I've erred
If where I've placed my hope is right
I need Your help – my heart is heavy
I feel I'm losing sight.

I know you said
Joy comes in the morning
I'm so ready for the sun to shine.

Please show me something
To let me know
If the path we're on is right.

Also, show me the end to this season – this dark season of night.

Lord, I don't want to overlook
The blessings that are here
Please open my eyes to see what is true
Help me see things very clear.

I decided early in life
To put all my stock in You
Please show me quickly – I need to know
I need to see the face of TRUTH.

My Heart Speaks Through My Pen

My heart speaks through my pen
It says what I can't say.
The words come from somewhere else
I can't take the credit today.

When I try to speak
Sometimes my tongue gets tied.
Tied into knots
By the words that are inside.

I really would like to speak them out
But silence comes instead.
But with the help of my pen
Hopefully, I'll say what needs to be said.

My desire is that the words will help
Those to whom I write.
And to everyone who reads the words
I pray they will shed light.

I believe the words are given to me
I just simply write them down.
I believe they're sent to help someone
Maybe all of us somehow.

So as you read the words I've written
Please, remember what I said.
The words are coming from my heart
And my heart speaks through my pen.

LORD, HELP ME REMEMBER
.......don't let me forget.

Lord, help me remember
What You've done for me.
Just like you did for Moses
At the Red Sea.

It was impossible!
And we both knew.
It was over for us
If it wasn't for You!

We both faced the impossible
We didn't know what to do.
But we did what You told us
That was our breakthrough!

There are so many things
When I look back and see.
So much You worked out
For my family and me.

And I want to thank You
I want to remember each one.
I never want to forget
All the things that You've done.

You've preserved and protected us
And strengthened us too.
We wouldn't have made it
If it wasn't for You.

But after this time
Has long past away.
I don't want to forget
How You delivered - Today.

Just like the nine lepers
Who just walked away.
Did they forget?
Or did they choose not to say...

Thank You, my Lord
From the depths of my heart.
For delivering us - like you did Moses
When the Red Sea You did part.

You did the IMPOSSIBLE!

　　　Lord, help me remember
　　　　　　.........don't let me forget.

SEASONS OF TRIALS

One morning I woke up
And as soon as I opened my eyes.
The pressures of life surrounded me
My response was of no surprise.

We had been in a "season of trials"
Everyday seemed to be getting worse.
Everyday seemed to be so hard
I began to think we were cursed.

Then the Lord reminded me
Every day, every minute is a choice.
We navigate through life's circumstances
By His Word and with our voice.

I chose to continue
In what I knew was true.
Was I going to rejoice or not?
I knew what I had to do!

So for a while when I'd wake up
The first thing I would say.
Was, "I choose right now to rejoice!"
"This is the day the Lord has made!"

It wasn't long after that
That I began to see.
Life looks a little better
I saw it differently.

Even though things still were hard
There was an assurance that came to me.
I knew my Savior was still with me
And I am blessed - I am Abraham's seed.

The day came and I could see
The storm had finally past.
And He was with us through it all
I can see that clearly, looking back.

The devil will distort things
So we won't see things as we should.
Unless we see what God sees
We'll see only the bad - not the good.

When you're going through
A time that seems so bleak.
You must look through the eyes of faith
Then you'll see victory - not defeat.

The way you look through eyes of faith
And see things like He does.
Is to keep His Word before your eyes
You'll see clearly the depths of His love.

God wants us to succeed in life
He has the Master Plan.
We must be diligent to follow it
Or we'll end up in sinking sand.

So remember when you're going through
A time that seems so bleak.
Look through the eyes of faith
You'll see VICTORY - not defeat!

Remember Me, Oh Lord

Remember me, oh Lord
When everyone forgets.
It may not look like I'm doing much
But I'm really doing my best.

I feel as though I've been stripped
Of a lot of things that once were mine.
From savings to retirement
From my own car – to even my time.

I feel as though I have nothing sometimes
And no one really cares.
Life goes on all around me
All I can do sometimes is stare.

Stare and just wonder
How did it ever get this way.
Sometimes I just want to go somewhere
But the only choice I have is to stay.

I feel like a bird in a cage
Whose wings have been clipped and can't fly.
I stand at the window and look out
Sometimes I just want to cry.

I know my family loves me
But they can't understand what I'm going through.
There are things that they just expect from me
Never asking what I want to do.

Because I don't leave my house everyday
Some think what I do isn't work.
The only difference is I don't get paid
Knowing they think this really hurts.

They never actually say it
But their actions speak loud enough.
The decisions I've been forced to make
Are unfair - and are really tough.

When it comes down to it all
It's You I want to please.
I may not do it right sometimes
Just have mercy on me ......please.

I'm going to make mistakes
I wish I never would.
I don't want to hurt anyone
But I want to say "no" when I should.

Help me know when it's ok to say "no"
And when it's ok to say "yes."
I want to do what You want me to
Nothing more - and nothing less.

It's been an honor and a privilege
To raise my own children these past several years.
It was my heart's desire to be at home with them
I've been living an answered prayer.

I know I have a lot more than some
I'm not meaning to complain.
Please allow me to be honest with You
Let me share what's on my heart today.

There's a situation that's come up
It needs to be worked out fast.
Lord, You know what's in my heart
Before I even ask.

I pray that it would work out
For everyone involved.
None of us know what to do
It's a problem only you can solve.

Please hear my cry! Please hear my heart!
Heal the hurts that I have caused.
Touch each one in my family
Let Your blessings on each one fall.

Also, remember the desires of my heart
Lord, hear me - answer when I call.

Oh, Lord, ...remember me.

Oh, Bonnie Isle of Scotland

Oh, Bonnie Isle of Scotland
You've been away from Me so long
I've never, ever quit loving you
But your resistance to Me is strong.

The time has come again to choose
You've rejected Me in the past
It's my Spirit that's been calling you
To come to Me at last.

My desire is that you all will come
And let Me be your God
The void that's there – I will fill
The emptiness will be gone.

That emptiness is very deep
It's a place only I can fill
I am the only One, True Living God
I've always been – And I am still.

So in the coming days
You'll see things you've never seen
So open up your hearts
And get ready to receive.

The things that you will see
I'm bringing to you by one.
One that you would not have chosen
But I chose him to get this job done.

That job is to, one last time
Bridge that long time gap
Between Me and my beloved Scotland
I long to have you back.

I SAW A FIRE

I saw a fire I'd never seen
Sunday morning when you preached.
It seemed to jump right off of you
It seemed a new level had been reached.

★★★★★★★★★★★★★★★★★★★★★★★★★★★★★★★★★★

There are stages that a fire goes through
It gets hotter the longer it burns.
You're entering into a new stage
For My People My Heart Yearns.

The fire that burns is My Spirit.
The conditions have to be just right.
Just follow Me - I'll lead you
It's just a matter of time.

The time will come when I will burn
And the flame will be so hot.
Like a forest fire that runs so fast
A fire - almost impossible to stop.

My fire is a perfect fire
But it destroys things in its path.
Like sin, sickness and perversion of My Word
These things kindle the flame of My wrath.

But after the fire has past
It leaves purity in its place.
It makes room for things to grow
I will fill the empty space.

So in the coming days
There will be more that you will learn.
That will make the conditions right for Me
Just right for Me to burn.

These words aren't meant to puff up
But to prepare for things to come.
I must be able to burn through men
Pray - "Not mine, but His will be done."

A STRANGER WE MEET

Through life's journey
We come across
Many people along the way.

Some we never see again
But others, in our hearts - they stay.

I believe there is a reason
For every path we cross.
Sometimes we know the reason
Sometimes, maybe not.

I believe there was a reason
That you crossed our paths that night.
You enriched our lives, by just being there
I believe the timing was just right.

There was a connection that we felt
You are in our hearts to stay.
We want you to know we care for you
And for you, we will earnestly pray.

Pray that your eyes will be opened
To anything you need to see.
We pray God's blessings be upon you
And on your family.

God truly loves you
What He says – is true.
Just ask Him to be your God
And He'll show Himself real to you.

Sometimes the most wonderful things in life
Can't be reasoned or explained.
Just simply believe what they are
And be thankful for them today.

He and I were once strangers
Until my path He crossed.
Since then, He's been my best friend
Without Him – I'd be lost.

*That stranger we meet..........
could change our lives forever.

IT MATTERS WHAT'S IN YOUR HEART

It matters what's in your heart
For that is where I live.
I know exactly what is there
What's in there, is what you'll give.

If I am only there
Power and love will flow.
But if there are obstructions
The Living Water cannot flow.

If you're not sure, at the time
If anything's in the way.
There's one true test - Ask yourself
Did God's presence leave or did it stay?

You may not always feel Me there
But there will always be signs.
Where I'm present, peace will reign
And I leave no man behind.

I love everyone
No matter what they've done.
Man cannot redeem himself
That's why I sent my Son.

Sometimes it will be hard
To do what you should do.
But just remember what I did
And how much I loved you.

At times you may think
You must act to do My will.
Sometimes all that I require
Is that you simply just be still.

Be careful that along the way
You don't fall into the trap.
The trap of proving that you're right
It will only set you back.

I will judge what's right and wrong
For I am the Righteous Judge.
Man does not always see things clear
Remember how they judged My Son?

But when he was wronged, he said nothing

        ....but,

"Father, forgive them, for they know not what they've done."

I love Him so very much
And I love you so much, too.
Keep on going – Full speed ahead!
There's still much I need you to do.

So just stay focused – I'm still here
Just listen to MY lead.
I'll get you where you need to go
Just keep your eyes on Me.

"Guard you heart with all diligence........

             IT MATTERS WHAT'S IN YOUR HEART

I've seen how...........

Kindness

Spreads So

Sweetly

What I've Learned

A precious lady asked me on my birthday
"What have you learned this past year?"
I stopped and thought - but couldn't answer then
I wanted my answer to be sincere.

I said to her, "I'll get back to you."
And we went on to other things.
But that question wouldn't leave me
So, I set some time aside to think.

As I sat early at my table
To write what came to mind.
I realized I had learned a lot
In that period of time.

I've learned there is a perfect order
In everything we do.
To get a successful outcome
There are certain things that we must do.

To get a desired outcome
We don't leave it all to chance.
You can see that this is true
Even in growing plants.

If you leave a plant to itself
And hope that it will live.
Without the proper care
It's chances are pretty slim.

I've learned life is about the same
We must give it proper care.
By following life's instructions (God's Word)
And maintaining it with prayer.

Some say they don't believe in prayer
But I've seen it work too many times.
Yes, I, too, have been disappointed
And found myself asking, "why?"

But, I wouldn't say that gardening doesn't work
Because some of my plants have died.
I'd just be more determined
To find out the reason why.

I've learned that perseverance PAYS OFF!
And things do change when we pray.
I've learned I shouldn't stop believing
Even when things don't go my way.

I've learned that unforgiveness is a destroyer
And it imprisons the one it holds.
I've seen how kindness spreads so sweetly
I believe what a man reaps is what he sows.

So, I must thank the one who asked me that day
That question I, too, will pass on.
"What did you learn this past year?"

.........I've learned ONLY good
Is what I want to pass on.

EVERY IDLE WORD

Every idle word will be answered for on Judgment Day
Help me to choose carefully
Every word I say.

For every word has a mission
As soon as it's spoken out.
Lord put a guard on my lips
Before anything bad slips out.

As your words exit your mouth
They carry a power unseen.
They will set things into motion
Even the words you say you don't mean.

For every word that is spoken
It leaves life or a very deep wound.
That somehow lasts a very long time
It's not forgotten anytime soon.

Take a minute to think about
The words that have been spoken to you.
They could have been spoken years ago
But the words still ring very true.

Some of these words - they lifted us high
Others brought us so low.
Some of those words - they cut like a knife!
Some brought peace to our sad weary soul.

Ask for forgiveness if wrong things were said
If they we're said, that's what we must do.
But it's better if we don't say them at all
For sometimes they leave residue.

Lord,
    Forgive me for every idle word I've spoken.

But I say unto you, That every idle word that men shall speak, they shall give account thereof in the day of judgment. Matthew 12:36

A MONSTER AMONG US

When things go good
There's usually a sweetness in the air.
But when things don't go our way
The monster rears it's ugly head.

It disguises itself so cunningly
Behind sweet empty words.
Until someone does something we don't like
Then viciousness is all that's heard.

All of a sudden we start pointing fingers
And the "blame game" usually starts.
We tell them how wrong they are
And that everything is "their" fault.

This monster - It lies dormant
Waiting to manifest through us all.
Unless it's replaced with what can kill it
The Presence of Almighty God.

This monster - it is pride!
It's selfishness at its peak!
It rises and takes over
When the main subject is "I" and "me".

This monster it can destroy
So many wonderful things.
Like friendships, churches, businesses, marriages
It's favorite is the family.

If you never say "I'm sorry"
If you never say "I'm wrong."
It's probably because in your heart
Pride has made its home.

We have to outsmart it
We must not let it win.
We must choose to refuse it
And walk in love until the end.

When we choose to walk in love
We put others before ourselves.
That's when the monster starts to die
In its clutches – we can no longer be held.

Now don't get me wrong
We have to deal with things in life.
We have to talk things out sometimes
But don't be pushed around by pride.

At times, I've been held captive
By this ugly monster 'pride'.
But when I chose God's weapon "love"
I've watched the monster die.

Don't allow pride…......a monster among us.

…………...WALK IN LOVE..

A PERFECT PLAN
......worked through imperfect people.

Don't gauge God's plan
Based on perfection
From you and me.

It's based on one's willingness
To fulfill His plan.
Not based on what
You or I might see.

He said the "just "will live by faith
And only by His Spirit we must be led.
Otherwise we'll be tossed to and fro
By double mindedness instead.

If we are double minded we cannot expect
To receive anything from God.
He's not withholding to be mean
Like gravity - It's just a law.

So when we see someone
And we don't think they meet the mark,
Quickly ask forgiveness
For that being in your heart.

To think that way about someone
Is just lifting "yourself" up.
That kind of thinking is from below
It doesn't come from above.

So we must humble ourselves before Almighty God
And ask what "we" should do.
And on life's journey, don't criticize others
Because they're not like you.

Gods plan is a perfect plan
He wants to use us all.
But the truth is there are few
That will ever answer His call.

So as we walk along in life
Do all that "you" can
Don't focus on what others "aren't"
Be focused on God's plan.

........A PERFECT PLAN
worked through imperfect people.

Don't Judge!

THE BLESSING OF THE LORD

The Blessing of the Lord is rich
The Blessing of the Lord is free.
The only requirement - Surrender, Obedience.
To the Lord from you and me.

It brings with it no sorrow
With wings it will not flee.
It's what God intended for us all
When Christ died on Calvary.

When I look at your family
I see that you are blessed.
The Hand of the Lord is upon you
I see nothing, but God's best.

I've known you'll for a long time
I've seen how you live.
You live life for Him - humbly
And are always willing to give.

Your lives are a testimony
Of the Goodness of our God.
If we are just obedient to Him
And answer when he calls.

I pray you will have many
Happy years in your new home.
Thank you for your example and friendship
They mean more than you'll ever know.

When Two Lives Become One

When two lives become one
Things will start to change.
The strong become stronger
The weights of life are less of a strain.

That strain of carrying a heavy load
That's hard to carry all alone.
And those loving arms that will await you
When you finally make it home.

It is a blessing when you find
The one that you'll love.
"From this day forward"
To the end of all time.

This union was meant only
To bring nothing but good.
But we must cherish the other
The way that we should.

Love them - be honest
Be nothing, but true.
You'll see when you do this
It will come back to you.

Things won't be perfect everyday
But there is a comfort knowing.
Someone's always there for you
And by your side they'll stay.

Love, cherish and protect HER
She is worth more than precious jewels.
Love, comfort and encourage HIM
All the days of your life, do him good.

As you begin your lives new this day
I ask God's blessings upon you to stay.
May you be happy, healthy, prosperous too.
And also your children, the "precious two"!

Congratulations!
We love you'll!

ANOTHER DAY GONE BY

Another day has come and gone
And leaves me with this thought again.
Did I do today - All I could
According to His plan.

The sun will rise. The sun will set.
But there's much time in between.
To do the things that He wants done
Things done by you and me.

Sometimes the things are really big
Sometimes they're very small.
But they're all so important
In the scheme of it all.

There's no way we really know
What a difference it truly makes.
When we just obey the voice of God
It could mean a different path that someone takes.

It might be a quick phone call
Or coffee with a friend.
It might be simply listening
To bring someone's sadness to an end.

It could be going to work
Each and every day.
To be a good provider
For yourself and your family.

Or it could be something like
Taking a different job or moving to a new place.
Or "No matter how things look right now,
The right thing to do is stay."

Whatever it is we are to do
In this life each day.
We must tune in to the One who knows
To get our instructions for the day.

Lord, help me hear what I should do
Lord, help me see what I should see.
Help me move aside - as You step in
To help that one in need.

Lord, help me put to death each day
That selfish part in me.
The part that says, "I can't do that!"
Or, "I'm busy. Don't bother me!"

When others look at me
I pray it's YOU they'll see.
Whether it's a stranger or a friend
Or my family.

As we get out of bed each day
There are things we're each assigned.
So we can live life to the fullest
And it won't be just another day gone by.

Lord, help me live today to the fullest - doing all you have assigned to ME.
Don't let this be just another day..........

........just ANOTHER DAY GONE BY.

DOES IT REALLY MATTER?

Does it really matter
When you give your life to Him?
Does it matter if you honor your parents
Or try to choose the best of friends?

Does it matter the many times
That you chose to say "no."
To the things that would displease
The One who loves you so.

Does it matter that you try your best
Each and every day.
To please the One you cannot see
In hopes He'll one day say.

"Well done thou good and faithful servant."
I've watched you from day one.
No you were not perfect
That's why I sent My Son.

Yes….. It matters when you put me first
In everything you do.
I've promised to reward you
For good things you say and do.

For when you do the things I say
You prove your love for Me.
And great is My goodness
For them that worship Me.

Yes….. It really matters
When you choose to serve Me.
I promised great rewards to those
Who seek me diligently.

SUNRAYS AND SHADOWS

Sunrays and shadows
Send a message from above.
Though both of them are different
They're a sign of His great love.

The sunrays they remind us
Of the warmth sent on each ray.
And of the light He sends with it
So we can find our way.

The shadows, though sometimes dark
Send a message too.
When you step into its shade
Means He's protecting you.

Protecting when it gets too hot.
Or sometimes from life's stings.
In Psalm 36 verse 7
It's called the shadow of His wings.

So take a look
They're all around.
They originate from above.

Another gift
For His creation.
Another sign of His great love.

So if you're standing in the rays
Or the shadows of the shade.
Remember, He's with you in them both.
To see you're always safe.

SUNRAYS AND SHADOWS

....

A Signature of Love

A signature possesses something
That no other writing does.
It states what you've said is "true"
It means you'll keep your word.

The day of the hand shake
Seems to be long gone.
But the power of the signature
Still is holding on.

A signature is your character
It means you'll keep your word.
It means you'll keep your promises
Even if it's to your own hurt.

It also is a mark
That describes or stands for "you."
Like a singer with his hat
Or like Elvis' blue suede shoes.

Then there's the cross that signifies
The sacrifice that was made.
For all of mankind
That Jesus died to save.

The cross it shows the character
Of a selfless, loving God.
I don't know of anyone else
That would give their only son.

Give Him to be crucified
For a lost and sinful race.
For a chance to redeem them all
If they'll accept His Amazing Grace.

So every time we see a cross
Let's think of what God's done.
Let's realize what it stands for
It's His signature of Love.

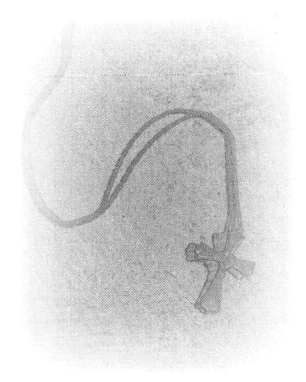

For You, From Me <3

This poem is for my children
I wondered when it would come.
I always thought it would be sooner
But, it's here now that I'm almost done.

Done with the book that was started
Many years in the past.
I guess since you're so special to me
The best was saved for last. ☺

I want each word to express
I want them clearly to convey.
Every day I've spent with you
Means more than I could say.

I remember the first day
That I held you in my arms.
Who knew such a little bundle
Could capture someone's heart.

There is also something I recall
That was *so much more* than sweet.
It's when I looked down into your eyes
And saw you looking back at me.

Jake, you were already bright-eyed
Emily, you were puckering for a kiss.
And every day since – has been an adventure
There's not a day that I would miss!

There are so many good memories
For me - that have been made.
From the first day of kindergarten
To the big "Graduation Day."

I've seen how you both have grown
Into adults today.
Adults with good, strong character
That will carry you the rest of the way.

I want you to know
I couldn't be prouder
Of you – And what you will do.

If you're happy
And doing your best every day,
What more could anyone ask of you?

You each have so much potential
Never stop short of the mark.
What you have to change your piece of the world
You'll find that down in your heart.

It's that thing that makes you happiest
Like no other thing can.
It's God that put that deep in there
It was all part of the plan.

So find that thing that fulfills you
As you're doing your work every day.
It might not always be easy
Ask Him – He'll show you the way.

And when the day comes
You have children of your own
You'll know what I said was true.

"I never thought I could
Love anyone so much.
That is – until I had you."

There are a few more "mom things"
I would like to say to you.
Remember, in EVERYTHING - put God first
Then, things will work out for you.

You've both been very sweet to me
In things you've said and what you've done.
I couldn't have asked for anything more
In a daughter or in a son.

As life goes on – always remember
With all my heart I've given my best.
Always know how much your mother loves you
Please, don't every forget.

                              Love,
                                    Mom

SCRIPTURE REFERENCES
(King James Version)

1. **Fresh New Beginnings**
2. **No Regrets** - Proverbs 18:21 Death and life are in the power of the tongue; and they that love it shall eat the fruit thereof., Lamentations 3:22 It is of the Lord's mercies that we are not consumed, because his compassions fail not. They are new every morning: great is thy faithfulness.
3. **So Much More Than That** - John 10:10 The thief cometh not, but for to steal, and to kill, and to destroy: I am come that they might have life, and that they might have it more abundantly.
4. **The Beauty of the Rose** – Ecclesiastes 3:11 He made ever thing beautiful in his time:...
5. **Our Mema**
6. **A Fan for Jesus** -Daniel 3, Mark 10, Matthew 14
7. **Seasons** - Ecclesiastes 3:1 To everything there is a season.......
8. **My Mouth Was Made For Praise** – Psalms 150:6 Let everything that hath breath praise the Lord. Praise ye the Lord., Matthew 12:34 ....for out of the abundance of the heart the mouth speaketh. Psalms 141:3 Set a watch, O LORD, before my mouth; keep the door of my lips.
9. **A True Giver** - Matthew 6:1-4

10. **Taking The Time** – Isaiah 55:8-9, Matthew 25:40 ....inasmuch as ye have done it unto one of the least of these my brethren, ye have done it unto me.

11. **Forgive Me**

12. **Just Five More Minutes** – Isaiah 54:17 No weapon formed against thee shall prosper:....

13. **Whispers From Heaven** – I Kings 19, Psalms 46:10 Be still, and know that I am God:...

14. **Yes, I Am Real** – Daniel 12:2, Matthew 25:46

15. **The Word** – Hebrews 4:12, James 1:21, John 1:14, Ephesians 5:26, Luke 8:11, II Peter 1:4, Psalms 12:6, Romans 15:4, Matthew 8:8, Psalms 119:105, Proverbs 4:22, Matthew 4:4, II Corinthians 6:7 Titus 1:9, Roman 10:8, Jeremiah 15:16, Hebrews 1:3, Luke 4:32, Proverbs 13:13, Colossians 3:16

16. **It Won't Be Long** – Revelation 22:12 And, behold, I come quickly; ...

17. **No Surprise To Me** – Jeremiah 29:11 For I know the thoughts that I think toward you, saith the Lord, thoughts of peace, and not of evil, to give you an expected end., Hebrews 13:5 ...I will never leave thee, nor forsake thee.

18. **Through My Kitchen Window**

19. **I Prayed For You Today** - John 10:10 The thief cometh not, but for to steal, and to kill, and to destroy: I am come that they might have life, and that they might have it more abundantly., Hebrews 13:8 Jesus Christ the same yesterday, and today, and forever.

20. **True Treasures**

21. **Questions of the Heart** – I John 4:19 We love him, because he first loved us.

22. **A Vessel of Honor** – II Timothy 2:20

23. **A Soul That's Lost Forever** - Matthew 25:41, John 14:16, Isaiah 3:24, Revelation 20, Revelation 14.

24. **Help Me Care Like You Care**

25. **The Water's Edge** – Psalms 23

26. **Keep Trusting In Me** – Proverbs 3:5 Trust in the Lord with all thine heart; and lean not unto thine own understanding. In all thy ways acknowledge him, and he shall direct thy paths., Hebrews 13:5 ...I will never leave thee, nor forsake thee., Galatians 6:9 And let us not be weary in well doing: for in due season we shall reap, if we faint not.

27. **When Your Back's Against the Wall** – Psalms 4:6, Psalm 89:15, II Samuel 22:29, Psalms 86:7, Psalms 91:15

28. **How Long Must I Wait** – Psalms 30:5 ....weeping may endure for a night, but joy cometh in the morning., Isaiah 40:31 But they that wait upon the Lord shall renew their strength;...

29. **My Heart Speaks Through My Pen**

30. **Lord, Help Me Remember** – Luke 17:11-19, Exodus 14:21

31. **Seasons of Trials** – Psalms 118:24 This is the day which the Lord hath made; we will rejoice and be glad in it., Romans 10:17 So then faith cometh by hearing, and hearing by the word of God., I John 5:4 ...and this is the victory that overcometh the world, even our faith.

32. **Remember Me, Oh Lord** – Psalms 61:1-4 Hear my cry, O God; attend unto my prayer. From the end of the earth will I cry unto thee, when my heart is overwhelmed; lead me to the rock that is higher than I.

33. **Oh, Bonnie Isle of Scotland**

34. **I Saw A Fire** – Luke 3:16, Hebrews 12:29, Psalms 89:46

35. **The Stranger We Meet**

36. **It Matters What's In Your Heart** – Proverbs 4:23 Keep thy heart with all diligence; for out of it are the issues of life.

37. **What I've Learned**

38. **Every Idle Word** – Matthew 12:36 But I say unto you, That every idle word that men shall speak, they shall give account thereof in the day of judgment.

39. **A Monster Among Us** – Proverbs 16:18 Pride goes before destruction, and a haughty spirit before a fall., Proverbs 29:3 One's pride will bring him low, but he who is lowly in spirit will obtain honor., Proverbs 11:2, Proverbs 16:5, James 3:6 ...AND THE TONGUE IS A FIRE,.....

40. **A Perfect Plan** – Romans 1:17 ....The just shall live by faith., James 1:8 A double minded man is unstable in all his ways., Matthew 7:1 JUDGE not, that ye be not judged.

41. **The Blessing of the Lord** – I Samuel 15:22 ...to obey is better than sacrifice..., Proverbs 10:22 The blessing of the Lord, it maketh rich, and he addeth no sorrow with it.

42. **When Two Lives Become One** - Proverbs 31, Ecclesiastes 4:9-12 Two are better than one; .... For if they fall, the one will lift up his fellow:..........

43. **Another Day Gone By**

44. **Does It Really Matter?** – John 14:15 If you love me, keep my commandments., Hebrews 11:6 ...He is a rewarder of them that diligently seek Him.

45. **Sunrays and Shadows** – Psalms 91, Psalms 36:7 How excellent is thy loving-kindness, O God! Therefore the children of men put their trust under the Shadow of thy wings., Psalm 121:5, Proverbs 16:15

46. **Signature of Love** – John 3:16 For God so loved the world, that He gave His only begotten Son, that whosoever believeth in Him should not perish, but have everlasting life.

47. **For You, From Me**

Printed in the United States
By Bookmasters